eat smart

Dairy

Vic Parker

QED

Quarto is the authority on a w...
Quarto educates, entertains a...
our readers—enthusiasts an...
www.quartoknows.com

Ask an adult for help

Always ask an adult to help you make the recipes and get all the ingredients and equipment ready. Remember to wash your hands before you start.

Publisher: Maxime Boucknooghe
Editorial Director: Victoria Garrard
Art Director: Miranda Snow
Design and Editorial: Starry Dog Books Ltd
Consultant: Charlotte Stirling-Reed BSc (hons), MSc, RNutr (Public Health)

Words in **bold** are explained in the glossary on page 22.

Picture credits
(t=top, b=bottom, l=left, r=right, c=centre, fc=front cover)

Alamy Images fc D. Hurst, fc Sue Wilson, 7cr Robert Harding Picture Library Ltd, 7br Imagestate Media Partners Limited – Impact Photos, 9br Profimedia International S.R.O, 11c (yoghurt) Sue Wilson, 11bl (soy) D. Hurst, 11bc (c/cheese) D. Hurst, 14cr Nigel Cattlin, 15tr Ace Stock Ltd, 15cl Bon Appetit, 16br Paul Carter, 17bl (cheeses) FAN Travelstock, 17bl (m/red) Robert Morris, 17br (white) Robert Morris.

Corbis 4bl Digital Zoo, 5tl Ed Kashi, 6bl Little Blue Wolf Productions, 13bl Mark E Gibson, 17tl Massimo Borchi

Photolibrary 4br & 14tr Rosenfeld, 8cl & 14bl Fresh Food Images/David Marsden

Photoshot 7tr World Pictures, 16cl World Pictures/Colin Matthieu

Rex Features 12br, Gill Allen 14cl, 17cr.

Shutterstock fc Sharon Day, fc ampFotoStudio, fc Georgy Markov, fc Joao Virissimo, fc Ingvald Kaldhussater, fc Johanna Goodyear, fc Elena Schweitzer, fc Lepas, fc Eric Isselee, fc Tischenko Irina, fc AlenKadr, fc Evgeny Karandaev, 4tr Georgy Markov, 4cl Sharon Day (bottle), 4cl (cow) Gillian McRedel, 4cr (yog) nito, 4bl (bottle) ampFotoStudio, 5br (shake/fruits) Pinkcandy, 6c cdrin, 6bc Apostolos Mastoris, 6br (goat) Eric Isselée, 6-7 Martine Oger, 7tl Sebastian Knight, 7bl Iryna Rasko, 7bc AGphotographer, 8tl Tuomas Lehtinen, 8tr hacohob, 8c Hannamariah, 8bc Barbara Neveu, 8br Gelpi, 11tl (c/milk) Peter Zvonar, 11ct (g/milk) Jaimie Duplass, 12tr (bottle) Sharon Day, 12tr (cow) Gillian McRedel, 12cl Jean Frooms, 13tl Christopher Elwell, 13cr Tan Wei Ming, 13br Gillian McRedel,15bl Elena Schweitzer, 16tr Georgy Markov, 17bc (Welsh) Jeremy Smith, 17bc (creamy) Gregory Gerber, 19bl Eric Isselee, 19br Liv Friis-Larsen.

Nick Leggett 9l

Contents

Dairy products

Foods made from milk are called dairy products.

Cheese

There are many different types of dairy products, such as cheese, yoghurt and butter. The milk we drink may come from cows, goats, sheep and a few other animals.

Cow's milk

Yoghurt

Goat's milk

Butter

4

Milk is a liquid that contains millions of tiny drops of fat. To turn it into other dairy products, it is heated, cooled, shaken or has other ingredients added to it.

Sometimes the drops of fat in milk rise to the top, forming a separate layer. This is called cream.

Make a fruity milkshake

Ingredients:

- 1 ripe banana
- 80 g blueberries
- 160 ml **skimmed milk**
- 40 g strawberries

Makes: 1 serving

 1 Blend the banana and blueberries. Then add the milk and blend until the mixture is smooth.

 2 Add the strawberries and blend them in.

 3 Pour into a tall glass and enjoy!

Milk around the world

People around the world drink milk from many types of animal.

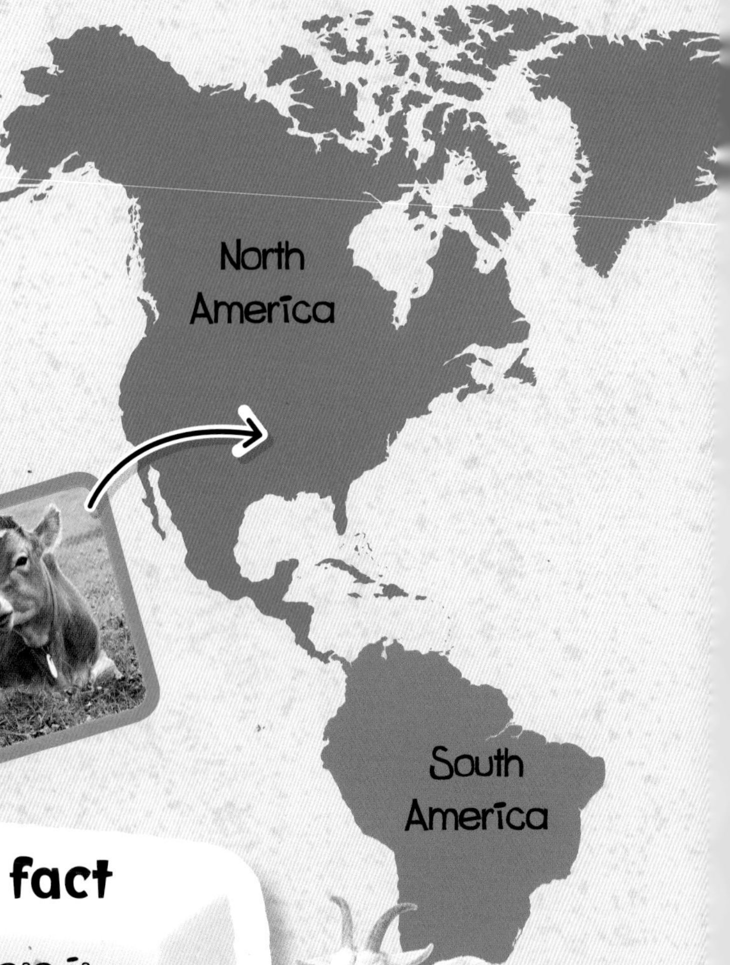

The various milks taste different, and some are creamier than others.

The United States is the second-largest milk producer in the world after India.

North America

South America

Food fact

Feta cheese is made from a mixture of goat's and sheep's milk.

Sheep

Goat

In many parts of Europe, people keep goats and sheep for their milk.

In central Asia, a yoghurt drink called kefir is made from horse's milk.

In the Himalayan region, **yak's** milk is used to make a cheese called chhurpi.

Europe

Asia

Africa

Oceania

In parts of Asia, people milk buffaloes. India has 75 million dairy farms, but most have fewer than 10 cows.

In Africa's deserts, **nomads** have made yoghurt and cheese from camel's milk for thousands of years.

In Italy, soft, white mozzarella cheese is made from the milk of water buffaloes.

Dairy products in meals

For a snack we might have cottage cheese on a cracker.

We eat dairy products in hot and cold meals, and as snacks.

 For breakfast we often have cereal with milk.

For lunch we might eat tomato soup with a spoonful of Greek yoghurt.

 For dinner we might fill a baked potato with cottage cheese.

For dessert we could have rice pudding, made with milk.

Ingredients:

- 2 tbsp Greek yoghurt
- 1 dessert spoon soft cheese (such as Mascarpone)
- 1 small tin of fruit cocktail
- 1 satsuma, chopped
- (optional) Ice cream cone

Makes: 1 serving

Make a tutti-frutti

1 Put the Greek yoghurt and soft cheese into a bowl and mix them together.

2 Stir in the fruit cocktail and chopped satsuma pieces.

3 Put the bowl in the fridge and leave to chill.

4 Serve, either in a glass or an ice cream cone, and enjoy!

When milk is kept in a warm place, it soon turns **sour**. Keeping milk cold in a fridge helps it to stay fresh for longer.

Dairy products such as yoghurt and milk need to be kept in the fridge.

Dairy products for a healthy body

Dairy products contain lots of nutrients that your body needs.

Cow's milk contains the mineral zinc, which helps our **immune system** to work properly.

Dairy products such as yoghurt contain **protein,** which our bodies need to grow and repair.

Cheese and other dairy products contain **calcium,** which makes our teeth and bones strong, and keeps our nerves and muscles healthy.

Cow's milk

Milk contains magnesium, which helps our muscles to work.

Goat's milk

Some people who can't drink cow's milk might choose an alternative, such as goat's milk.

Food fact

Some people, known as vegans, choose not to eat meat, eggs or dairy products. Instead of drinking milk from animals, they drink soy milk, made from soy beans, or almond milk.

Soy milk

Yoghurt

Yoghurt contains protein, which can help us to feel fuller for longer after we've eaten.

Soy beans

Cottage cheese

Cottage cheese contains less fat than many cheeses, so it is healthier for some people.

Milking cows

Cow's milk

Soon after a cow has had a baby calf, she starts producing milk for the calf to drink.

1 Farmers take the cows' milk for us to drink too. They milk the cows in a large shed called a milking parlour, where the cows are fed.

Dairy workers attach milking machines to the cows' **teats**. The machines pump the milk into large containers.

2

3 After being milked, the cows are taken back to their fields.

4

At the dairy, cream is taken off some of the milk to make skimmed and semi-skimmed milk. Unskimmed milk is called whole milk.

5 The cream and milks are then packaged and taken to shops to be sold.

Food fact

One dairy cow produces about 16 litres of milk a day, and 5840 litres of milk in a year.

Making butter

Butter

Butter is made from cream, which is the fattiest part of milk.

1 First the cream is heated to kill any harmful **bacteria** in it. This is called pasteurization.

2 Next, the cream is put in a churning machine. This makes the fatty part of the cream separate from the liquid part.

3 The fatty part of the cream clumps together and becomes solid chunks of butter.

The butter is packaged in plastic tubs or wrapped up in special paper. Then it is sent to shops to be sold.

4

5 The leftover liquid part of the cream is called buttermilk. It can be used in baking, and some people like to drink it.

Ingredients:

- 750 ml double cream

Make a pat of butter

1 Put the cream into a food processor and beat well on a high setting. The cream will gradually thicken into stiff whipped cream. When this happens, turn the speed down to low.

2 A few seconds later, a chunk of yellow butter will separate from the liquid. Turn off the food processor.

3 Drain off the liquid and knock the butter into a block or 'pat' using a flat spatula.

Making cheese

Cheese

There are many different types of cheese, but they are all made in four simple steps.

Step 1: Milk has bacteria added to it. Then it is heated. This makes the milk separate into solid curds and liquid whey.

Step 2: Some of the whey is drained off. If a lot of whey is removed, the cheese will be hard. If less is drained off, the cheese will be soft.

Step 3: The curds are poured into moulds that give the cheese its shape.

Step 4: The cheese is left to develop its flavour. This is called ripening. Some cheeses ripen in a few hours, but others take several years.

When it is ripe, the cheese is packaged and taken to shops to be sold.

Welsh Cheddar

White Cheddar

Mild red Cheddar

Food fact

Cheddar is the world's most popular cheese. There are more than 250 different types of Cheddar cheese.

Make yoghurt cheese

You will need:

- 500 ml Greek yoghurt
- Large, clean piece of thin cloth, such as **muslin**
- Ball of string
- Long stick
- Large mixing bowl
- Wholemeal bread

It's easy and fun to make your own cheese from yoghurt.

Put the yoghurt in the middle of the thin cloth or muslin.

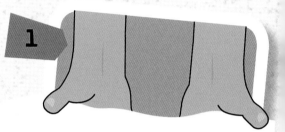

1

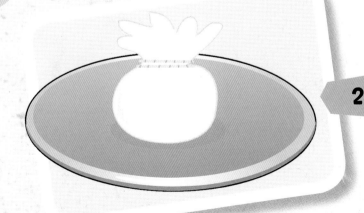

2 Bring the ends of the cloth together and tie the bundle with string so the yoghurt does not leak out.

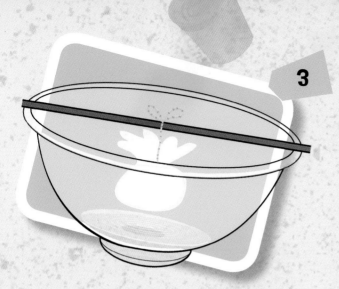

3 Tie the bundle to a stick. Place the stick across a mixing bowl so the bundle hangs down. Let all the whey from the yoghurt drip into the bowl.

When the whey has stopped dripping, untie the string. Roll the yoghurt cheese into small balls and serve them with some wholemeal toast.

4

Food fact

Greek yoghurt is usually made from sheep's milk, but it can also be made from cow's milk.

Greek yoghurt

Make cheesy red peppers

Try making this delicious recipe topped with gooey cheese!

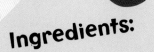

Ingredients:

- 50 g long grain rice
- 2 red peppers, cut in half with the seeds removed
- 1 tbsp olive oil
- 125 g Cheddar cheese, grated
- 1 small onion, chopped or diced
- 1 large egg, beaten
- 1 tsp English mustard
- 1 tbsp Worcestershire sauce

Makes: 4 servings

1

Ask an adult to set the oven to 190°C/375°F/Gas 5. Then put the rice into a sieve and rinse it well.

2 Tip the rice into a saucepan and fill the pan with water. Ask an adult to cook the rice on a low heat for about 10 minutes.

Put the pepper halves onto a baking tray and drizzle on some olive oil. Ask an adult to cook them in the oven for 15 minutes.

3

4 Drain the cooked rice and put it in a bowl. Stir in the cheese, chopped onion, egg, mustard and Worcestershire sauce.

Fill the pepper halves with the mixture. Ask an adult to put them back in the oven to cook for another 15 minutes. Then serve!

5

Glossary

Bacteria
Tiny living things. Bacteria are so small that they can only be seen through a microscope.

Calcium
A nutrient that helps to make your bones and teeth strong.

Immune system
Parts of the body that work together to fight off sickness and protect the body.

Muslin
A very fine cotton fabric.

Nomads
People who have no fixed home, but instead travel from place to place in search of food, water and grazing for their animals.

Protein
A substance in foods that helps the body to grow and repair itself.

Skimmed milk
Milk that has had the cream removed from it.

Sour
A sharp, unpleasant taste.

Teats
The parts of a female animal's body that her babies suck on to drink milk.

Yak
A type of cattle with long hair and long horns.

Index

Next steps

❉ Show the children pictures of a variety of foods and pick out which ones are dairy foods. Discuss how each dairy product is made.

❉ Talk about why our bodies need dairy foods to stay healthy and how much we should eat every day.

❉ Discuss why low-fat dairy foods are healthier choices than full-fat ones. Make a picture list of how we might choose low-fat dairy foods instead of full-fat ones. For example, choosing to have low-fat yoghurt with fresh fruit for dessert, instead of fruit with cream.

❉ Make a poster of cheeses from around the world, showing their names and what milk they are made from.

❉ Look for recipes for making your own yoghurt. You can either use a yoghurt-making machine or you can keep the milk in a warm place – this will work just as well. Use full-fat milk and a few teaspoons of plain, live, whole milk yoghurt as a starter. Add fruit and flavourings to make different kinds of yoghurt.

❉ Talk about how we might use different types of dairy food in cooking. Make an international dairy cookbook with recipes and pictures from around the world.